Amanda —
We'll miss you —
but wish you —
well in your new
adventures! Keep
reading! Best —
Sally

Amanda,
I so enjoy
being with
in the book
will really
you!
XOL
Andrea

Amanda dear,
I am to sorry that
you are leaving Santa Fe
and our women's book group.
You know that I was looking
forward to knowing you better
and spending more time together.
Alas work got in the way.
Best of Luck,
XX Judy

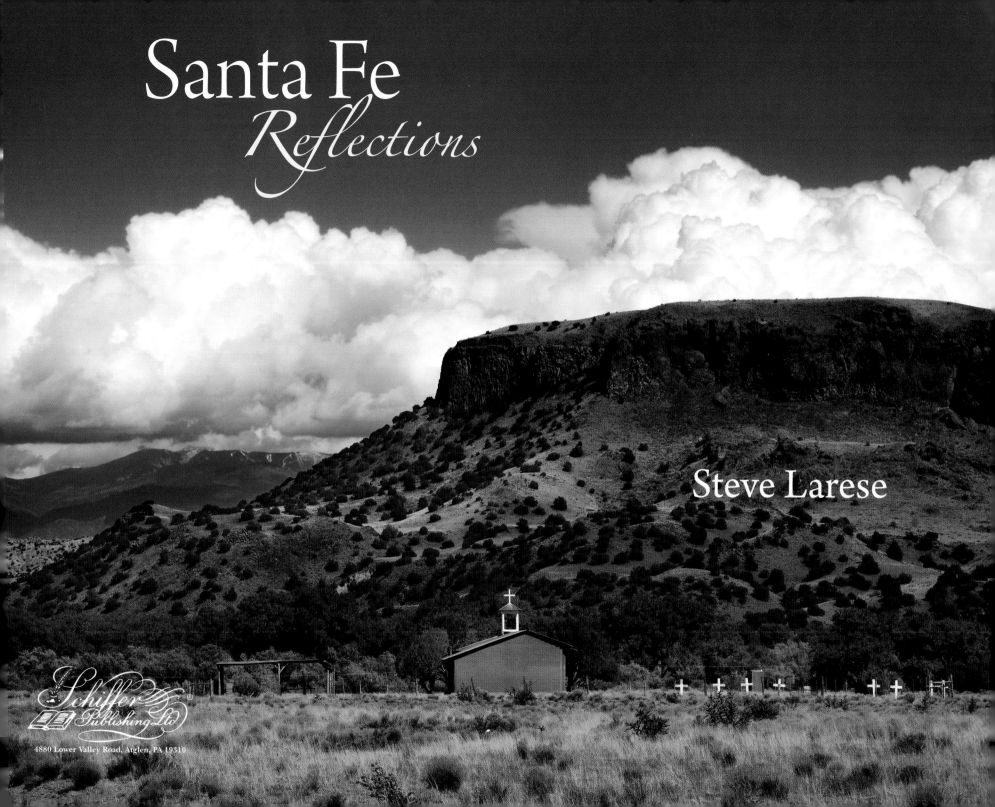

Santa Fe
Reflections

Steve Larese

Schiffer Publishing Ltd®

4880 Lower Valley Road, Atglen, PA 19310

Another Schiffer Book By The Author:
Durango Perspectives. ISBN:978-0-7643-3337-8. $9.99

Cover and book designed by: Bruce Waters
Type set in Zurich BT

ISBN: 978-0-7643-3653-9
Printed in China

Schiffer Books are available at special discounts for bulk purchases for sales promotions or premiums. Special editions, including personalized covers, corporate imprints, and excerpts can be created in large quantities for special needs. For more information contact the publisher:

Published by Schiffer Publishing Ltd.
4880 Lower Valley Road
Atglen, PA 19310
Phone: (610) 593-1777; Fax: (610) 593-2002
E-mail: Info@schifferbooks.com

For the largest selection of fine reference books on this and related subjects, please visit our web site at **www.schifferbooks.com**
We are always looking for people to write books on new and related subjects. If you have an idea for a book please contact us at the above address.

This book may be purchased from the publisher.
Include $5.00 for shipping.
Please try your bookstore first.
You may write for a free catalog.

In Europe, Schiffer books are distributed by
Bushwood Books
6 Marksbury Ave.
Kew Gardens
Surrey TW9 4JF England
Phone: 44 (0) 20 8392 8585; Fax: 44 (0) 20 8392 9876
E-mail: info@bushwoodbooks.co.uk
Website: www.bushwoodbooks.co.uk

Contents

Introduction

Cultural, creative, chic and historic, Santa Fe lives up to its sobriquet as the City Different. Whether it's snow blanketing sensual adobe walls, spring flowers splashing the Plaza, fiestas lasting long into warm summer nights or reds and gold dripping from aspens in the surrounding Sangre de Cristo Mountains, Santa Fe is uniquely suited for every season. This book records reflections of the annual seasons in and around Santa Fe.

A Little History

La Villa Real de Santa Fe - the Royal Town of Santa Fe - was established by Spanish governor Don Pedro de Peralta in 1608-10, making the city the oldest continuous capital in what is now the United States. The Spanish entered New Mexico in 1540, 80 years before the pilgrims landed at Plymouth Rock in 1620. As Santa Fe moves past its 400th anniversary, it's heady to think about the changes New Mexico's capital has undergone, and at the same time how little has changed since the days of the conquistadors.

The charm, mystery and allure of Santa Fe are seen worldwide; even on a recent stay in the Dominican Republic my wife and I smiled at the Santa Fe Restaurant in Punta Cana, complete with an image of Canyon Road's iconic 304 doorway on the menu. Car manufactures borrow the name, and chances are you've seen Santa Fe used in all manner of marketing representing the entire American Southwest. The name Santa Fe is used worldwide to evoke rugged beauty and grace. Beyond the Old West image many attribute to Santa Fe, the community is as diverse as the world. Artists, politicians, stars, wanderers, newcomers and those who trace their families back to Spain or before recorded time, people of many races and religions, all call Santa Fe home and co-exist in relative harmony. Santa Fe has always been a place for movers and mavericks, and one supports the other here.

Downtown Santa Fe

Much of Santa Fe is a walker's town, roads having been laid out over donkey paths (which can make driving interesting). To explore Santa Fe, start at its heart – the Plaza, which is listed on the National Registry of Historic Places. It has served as a beloved gathering place for residents of every walk of life for centuries. Grab a Frito pie or cup of coffee and find a bench under a shady tree; it's a wonderful place to relax and people watch. The center monument honors Federal soldiers who fought in New Mexico during the Civil War, and if you look closely you can find where, years later, a wayward bullet struck the obelisk. The bandstand is active year-round, especially summer nights when free outdoor concerts have the town dancing into the balmy night. Around the Plaza, humble adobe buildings were built. One of them, the **Palace of the Governors**, served as the capitol building for Spanish, Mexican and Territorial U.S. governors. Gov. Lew Wallace penned his epic book *Ben Hur* while serving here.

Today, the Palace of the Governors is a museum that displays more than 15,000 artifacts from the Spanish colonial (1540-1821), Mexican (1821-1846) and U.S. Territorial (1846-1912) periods of New Mexico's history. Weapons, armor, documents, clothing, furniture and items of daily life, from the Spanish through U.S. statehood in 1912, are proudly displayed. Outside, under the portal, Native American artisans representing many tribes sell their jewelry and pottery. Opened in May 2009, the **New Mexico History Museum** next to the Palace features interactive exhibits examining New Mexico's Native American, Spanish, Mexican, French and Anglo interactions and contributions.

At the nearby **New Mexico Museum of Art**, the works of early Santa Fe masters underscore how the city earned its international reputation as an artist's haven, and its ranking as the third-largest art market in the United States. In the 1920s, luminaries such as John Sloan, Andrew Dasburg and Russell Cheney trickled into Santa Fe, drawn by it magical light and easy living. Georgia O'Keeffe is honored with her own museum (**Georgia O'Keeffe Museum**) that features her bold and redefining work, as well as special showings of her contemporaries.

On Museum Hill, the **Museum of Indian Arts & Culture** highlights contemporary Native American art such as that of the late R.C. Gorman. The **Museum of International Folk Art** celebrates just that, amazing folk art from around the world. An entire room showcases thousands of clay figurines that depict Pueblo dances, complete with camera-wielding tourists, Mexican Day of the Dead celebrations and a scene of Heaven and Hell where even the devils look cheery. The nearby **Wheelwright Museum of the American Indian** and the **Museum of Spanish Colonial Art** display art, artifacts and furniture from New Mexico's Native American and Spanish history. At the State Capitol at Old Santa Fe Trail and Paseo de Peralta, don't miss the **Governor's Gallery** on the Fourth Floor, where contemporary artists from across New Mexico are featured. The **Capitol Art Collection**, displayed throughout the Roundhouse, is well worth exploring, with multimedia from New Mexican artists from every corner of the state.

Across Old Santa Fe Trail from the capitol, the **Barrio de Analco** is an ancient neighborhood that boasts both the oldest house and the oldest in-use church, San Miguel, in the United States (first built in 1610). Cute shops and cafés complete this charming area. Down Old Santa Fe Trail, as you approach the Plaza, is the Gothic chapel that houses the **Loretto Staircase** in Loretto Chapel. Called the "miraculous staircase" because of its lack of any central support, this wooden, spiral staircase uses no glue or nails, just wooden pegs and perfect carpentry. Built in the 1850s, legend has it that St. Joseph himself built it after the Sisters of Loretto prayed for help in their need to ascend to the choir loft.

The Art District

From pieces of hand-made Native American turquoise jewelry purchased directly from the artist to exquisite sculptures and paintings in galleries throughout the city, beautiful things abound in Santa Fe. Make sure to explore the side streets beyond the Plaza, as many shops filled with treasures are tucked away, waiting to be discovered. Strolling down **Canyon Road**, you may feel as though you're in a different city in the City Different. Dappled sunlight plays on warm adobe walls in classic Santa Fe style, but it's the contemporary art that glows from every surface that impresses both the causal viewer and connoisseur of fine art. More than 100 galleries in a square mile attract collectors worldwide, and make Canyon Road the largest concentration of art galleries per mile in the world. One of the best things serious shoppers can do for themselves in Santa Fe is to bring a good pair of walking shoes. When you need a break, enjoy the shade at **El Zaguan's Bandelier Garden**.

The Railyard

The **Railyard District**, just southwest of the plaza, is another exciting destination for art lovers. Modern warehouse-style galleries explore the newest in contemporary art, and the cafes, coffee shops, outdoor recreation stores and other businesses sprouting up around the **New Mexico Rail Runner** train station have made this area the newest hub for shopping, eating and strolling. It's easier than ever to travel between Santa Fe and Albuquerque by rail.

The nearby **Guadalupe District** is trendy with a Western twang, and is a destination for boutique shopping and bistro-style dining. Check out **Guadalupe Chapel**, the oldest extant church in the country, devoted to Our Lady of Guadalupe.

You'll work up an appetite with all of this exploring, and fortunately Santa Fe offers any fare that you crave. Romantic restaurants constantly garner international praise for their exciting blending of tastes from around the world. Almost always at the center of these creations is New Mexico chile. Many of the chefs have written their own cookbooks, so you can try their art at home.

Country Beyond the Town

Of course, Santa Fe wouldn't be the city it is without its natural beauty. At 7,000 feet, Santa Fe is cradled by aspen-covered mountains that provide a cool respite in the summer. In the fall, the mountains turn a blaze of yellows and reds, providing a striking backdrop for the city against the almost always brilliant blue sky. You can drive into this display by following **Hyde Park-Ski Basin Road**. At 8,300 feet, **Hyde Memorial State Park** is the gateway to the Santa Fe National Forest and the Pecos Wilderness. Come winter, Santa Fe offers some of the most rewarding skiing, snowboarding, snow-shoeing and cross-country skiing in the nation at the **Santa Fe Ski Area**. Near the end of Canyon Road is the trailhead for the **Dale Bale trail system**, a favorite of hikers and birders. **Winsor Trail** has been called one of the best mountain biking trails in the nation. Anglers, rafters and kayakers enjoy a watery playground on the nearby Río Grande. Santa Fe has several shops that specialize in hiking, biking, skiing, fly fishing and all other forms of outdoor recreation, and are a great place to glean tips on where to go.

For adventures of any flavor, from shopping to snowboarding, Santa Fe delivers in a way only this relaxing, romantic city can. I hope you enjoy these photographs that record a normal year in Santa Fe. See the region in four seasons on the following pages, and be inspired to visit soon, if you don't hang your hat here already.

Winter

A crescent moon rises above the Plaza
bedecked with holiday lights.

Cozy corner kiva fireplaces are ubiquitous in Santa Fe homes. Their name derives from Native American *kivas,* usually round, sunken rooms used for religious ceremonies that use similar fireplaces.

The Plaza's Soldier Monument was erected in 1866 as a American Indian War Memorial monument, honoring Federal troops killed in battles with both Confederate troops and Native Americans. Someone in the 1970s chiseled off the word "Savages".

January snow covers the Santa Fe Plaza, a National
Register of Historic Places location.

New Mexico's State capitol building, is called the Roundhouse for its circular structure with four wings, mirroring the state symbol that appears on the flag, the zia.

Canyon Road gate in snow.

The view from the corner of Water and Old Santa Fe Trail. Loretto Chapel is on the left.

East De Vargas Street looking east. This area, called the Barrio de Analco, has been a neighborhood since the early 1600s.

Looking east down San Francisco Street.

Descanso in snow. Descansos are crosses used to mark where a loved one has died, usually in a traffic accident. Originally, they marked where a casket was rested on the way to burial.

Climbers crest Santa Fe Baldy, a prominent peak in the Sangre de Cristo mountains north of Santa Fe. Called "baldy" because it rises above the tree line, it is 12,632 feet above sea level.

Sunset over a snowy land-
scape south of Santa Fe.

Camel Rock at Tesuque Pueblo north
of Santa Fe is aptly named.

Two views of the Loretto Chapel. Designed by French architect Antoine Mouly and built in the Gothic Revival style in 1878, it is most famous for its mysterious staircase. www.lorettochapel.com

The staircase in Loretto Chapel uses no nails, no supports and the wood is not found locally. It is essentially a perfectly built spring. When the chapel's designer suddenly died before the building was complete, the Sisters of Loretto realized they needed a way to the choir loft. Space was too limited for a traditional staircase, and a ladder would not be appropriate for the nuns. The Sisters prayed for a solution, and soon a mysterious carpenter showed up, and offered to build the staircase for no charge. Legend has it that the man was Joseph, the father of Jesus. Recent evidence supports the fact that the man was probably Frenchy Rocha, a wandering hermit who eventually died in Southern New Mexico in a cave.

Loretto Chapel interior

The Inn at Loretto uses Pueblo style in its design.

Snowboarding at Ski Santa Fe.

Santa Fe ski

Santa Fe homes nestle in the foothills of the Sangre de Cristo mountains. Moonrise over the Sangre de Cristos. The name is Spanish for "Blood of Christ" and refers to the pink hue the range takes on at sunset.

A door is decorated for the holidays.

In 1822, the famed Santa Fe Trail, a trade route from St. Louis, Missouri to New Mexico, ended at the Plaza. The "End of the Santa Fe Trail" marker was placed by the Daughters of American Revolution in 1911 and is on the southeast corner of the Plaza.

North of Santa Fe, Santuarió de Chimayó gets a December snow.

A starry night above Loretto Chapel.

The Inn at Loretto is well known for its holiday light display

A warm fire greets guest at the Inn at Loretto.

A Victorian Christmas at La Posada de Santa Fe.

Farolitos and gate. North of Albuquerque, bags filled with sand and candles are called farolitos – little lanterns. In Albuquerque and south, they are often called luminarias. Luminarias refer to small bonfires in Santa Fe.

Bella meets Santa Claus on the Santa Fe Southern Railway's Holiday Hotshot Train. The train offers a variety of ride year-round, most traveling to historic Lamy and back. www.sfsr.com

The Plaza with lights and snow.

Statue and farolitos.

People gather to sing carols on the Plaza.

Farolitos glow along Canyon Road on Christmas Eve.

Las Posadas reenacts the biblical story of Mary and Joseph looking for a room at an inn. Their attempts to find lodging are thwarted by the Devil. Finally, they are allowed to stay at the manger, in this case the courtyard of the Palace of the Governors. Mary and Joseph are followed by musicians and a crowd holding candles, as they are turned away by five dramatic devils throughout the Plaza.

The crowd follows Mary and Joseph around the Paza during Los Pasadas.

Devil Diana Maimin lets a young angel hold her pitchfork.

St. Francis Cathedral in snow.

Spring

A spring Santa Fe scene.

Flowers in a birdbath along Canyon Road celebrate spring.

Capitol with spring flowers. The capitol grounds display a wide
range of native trees and vegetation. (opposite)

31

Marigolds rival colorful art.

Ristras and flowers. Ristras are strings of chiles tied together to dry them for crushing into powder. They are also a favorite New Mexico decoration.

Wisteria, imported from the East Coast in the late 1800s, is a Santa Fe favorite.

Tulips herald spring along Washington Street.

Geraniums and vigas.

A giant ant sculpture welcomes guests to Canyon Road. This street is known for its many art galleries.

East Palace Avenue

Canyon Road has more than 100 galleries within its square mile, making it the highest concentration of art galleries anywhere in the world.

Artist Robert Anderson works *plein air*.

A Tibetan Buddha statue graces Canyon Road. Santa Fe has become home for displaced Tibetans who find the landscape similar to Tibet and appreciate the area's diverse cultures.

A friendly pedicab driver along Canyon Road.

Kinetic art uses wind power to create mesmerizing patterns along
Canyon Road.

Flowers and art along Canyon Road.

Painted cow skulls for sale.

A Canyon Road scene.

Ristras are ever-present in Santa Fe.

Flags are placed at graves at the Santa Fe National Cemetery every Memorial Day.

Art from India and other parts of the world mesh brilliantly with Santa Fe style.

Cart and flowers.

41

Summer

June 14 sees Santa Fe decorated with flags and bunting for Flag Day.

The Santuarío de Chimayó, about 30 miles north of Santa Fe, is famous for its Good Friday pilgrimages. In the days before Easter, thousands of people can been seen walking the roads from Santa Fe to Chimayó. Built in 1810, the site is revered for its alleged curative properties. Visitors may take a small scoop of dirt from a small room in the church.

The Sancuarió de Chimayó interior and alter underwent massive restoration in the early 2000s.

Every Good Friday, an estimated 30,000 people walk varying distances to Chimayó as a form of penitence.

Pilgrims stop to pray at cross along the way to Chimayó.

Votive candels, Chimayó.

A Chimayó lowrider airbrushed with the Stations of the Cross.

Sunset red rock landscape, south of Santa Fe.

El Rancho de las Golondrinas, south of Santa Fe, is a living history museum that features different aspects of New Mexico's history throughout the year. One of its most popular series is the Civil War re-enactment that takes place every May. www.golondrinas.org

The Institute of American Indian Art's Spring Homecoming Pow wow every May is a celebration of Native American culture. www.iaia.edu

49

The Santa Fe Depot enjoys a new life as the final destination of the New Mexico Rail Runner, a commuter train that travels from Santa Fe to Belén along the Interstate 25 corridor.

The Rail Runner leaves Santa Fe with the Sangre de Cristo mountains in the background.

Interstate 25 at night looking toward Santa Fe, with the Rail Runner lights in the median.

River rafting on The Rio Grande is a popular sport.

Jeméz Falls in the Santa Fe National Forest, west of Santa Fe, is a popular recreation area.

Opposite. Former New Mexico governor Gary Johnson takes on the rapids of The Rio Grande, north of Santa Fe.

The Rodeo! de Santa Fe, begun in 1949, is a Professional Rodeo Cowboys Association sanctioned event and is considered one of the top 100 rodeos in the nation. Perhaps even more popular is the parade kicking off the event, which travels through downtown Santa Fe. www.rodeodesantafe.org

A cowgirl wrangles a dinosaur during the Rodeo! de Santa Fe parade. The annual rodeo is every June.

Young mariachis in the Rodeo! de Santa Fe parade.

Calf roping during the Rodeo! de Santa Fe. Competitive events include individual and team roping, steer wrestling, barrel racing, saddle and bareback bronc riding and bull riding. www.rodeodesantafe.org

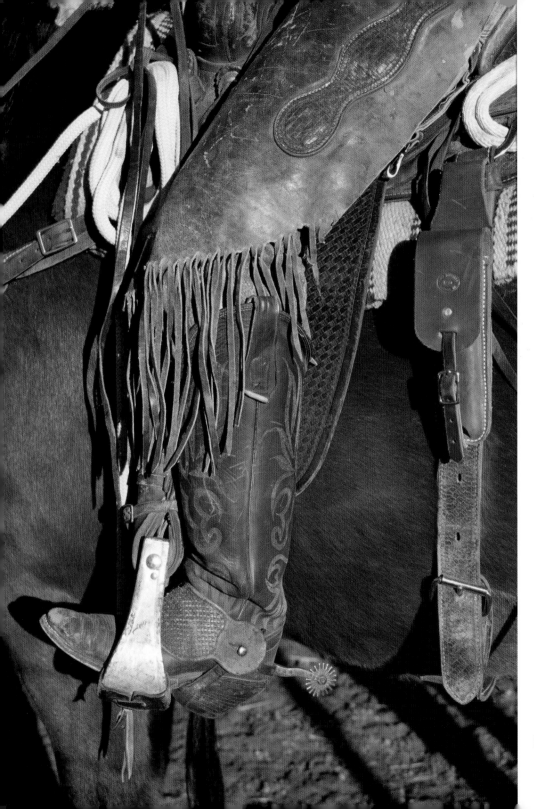

Above. Traditional Spanish Market celebrates Hispanic art every July on the Plaza. www.spanishmarket.org

Left. A Santa Fe cowboy sits tall in the saddle.

Since 1951, Traditional Spanish Market has taken place on the Plaza. Today there are two markets, one for traditional artforms and another for contemporary Spanish art. Winter Spanish Market is another event that takes place in December in the Santa Fe Convention Center. www.spanishmarket.org

Begun in 1922, the annual Santa Fe Indian Market showcases juried talent from Native American tribes from across North America. It is the largest and most prestigious Native American arts show in the world, and brings thousands of serious collectors to Santa Fe from around the world. Pottery, jewelry, paintings, clothing and traditional outfit contests are part of the weekend event, held each August. Many of the artists are able to make their year's salary at this event. www.swaia.org. (above and next 3 pages)

Top-quality Native American art brings collectors
to Santa Fe year-round.

Santa Fe is know worldwide for its fine dining,
including Mark Miller's Coyote Café.

Autumn

Autumn begins to tinge Santa Fe.

Santa Fe shares the top art market in the nation with New York and Los Angeles.

An autumn afternoon concert on the Plaza.

Santa Fe busking

Plaza summer night

Snow begins to dust the Sangre de Christos in fall.

Santa Fe from Cross of the Martyrs

A view south from La Fonda Hotel. Loretto Chapel
can be seen in the middle of the frame.

Once the home of poet Witter Bynner, the Inn of the Turquoise Bear is a bed and breakfast today. Guest of Bynner's who have stayed here include D.H. Lawrence, Willa Cather, Ansel Adams, Igor Stravinsky, Edna St. Vincent Millay, Robert Frost, W.H. Auden, Stephen Spender, Aldous Huxley, Clara Bow, Errol Flynn, Rita Hayworth, Robert Oppenheimer and Georgia O'Keeffe. Santa Fe has many small historic inns. www. nmbba.org

Santa Fe custom boots.

Ladder and adobe.

Since the 1930s, The Museum of New Mexico's Palace of the Governors Native American Vendor Program has allowed New Mexico tribal members to sell their work directly to the public, ensuring its authenticity and allowing buyers to meet the artists.

Flourish is added to a service door downtown.

Doors of Santa Fe.

A Santa Fe market.

Cart with flowers.

Adobe wall.

Old truck and painted barn, north of Santa Fe.

Flowers along Canyon Road.

Country singer and Santa Fe resident Randy Travis films a video in the Santa Fe's historic Rosario Cemetery.

Rainbow and Sangre de Cristo mountains, north of Santa Fe.

Window detail.

The original front door of the Stabb House. The resort has been built around the original structure. Note the initials AS above the door, for Abraham Stabb.

La Posada Resort and Spa was originally the home of Abraham and Julia Stabb, wealthy merchants who built their Victorian mansion in 1882. A German-Jewish pioneer, Abraham arrived in Santa Fe in 1858. After the death of a child, Julia sank into a deep depression and died in 1896. There are many accounts of her spirit being seen on the property. It became a hotel in the 1930s, and today is a luxury resort.

Stabb House, circa 1885.

Life imitates art in the streets of Santa Fe. The building is the La Fonda de Santa Fe, a historic hotel at the end of the Santa Fe Trail that is still a popular gathering spot for locals.

Santa Fe street scene in front of the Palace of the Governors.

Santa Fe's Scottish Rite Temple was built in 1911 and incorporates Moorish Revival architecture, after the Court of the Lions at the Alhambra in Spain.

La Fonda has a colorful interior, and many of the windows have been painted by staff artist Ernesto Martinez. Called the Living Room of Santa Fe, many famous and infamous people have met and stayed at the hotel, which is listed on the National Trust Historic Hotel of America.

La Fonda in the 1930s

La Fonda (Spanish for "Inn") has been a hotel and social gathering spot since Santa Fe was founded in 1607. Undergoing many redesigns over the centuries, the current structure was built in 1922, right at the end of the Santa Fe Trail. In 1925 it was leased to Fred Harvey, who made it one of his famous Harvey Houses, until 1968.

Cathedral Park.

The Cathedral Basilica of Saint Francis of Assisi, commonly known as Saint Francis Cathedral, was built in 1869 under the direction of Archbishop Jean-Baptiste Lamy.

Abraham and Julia Stabb were friends of Bishop Lamy. Although they were Jewish, they donated money to the construction of the Catholic Church. In appreciation, Bishop Lamy had the Hebrew Tetragrammaton placed above the cathedral's main door.

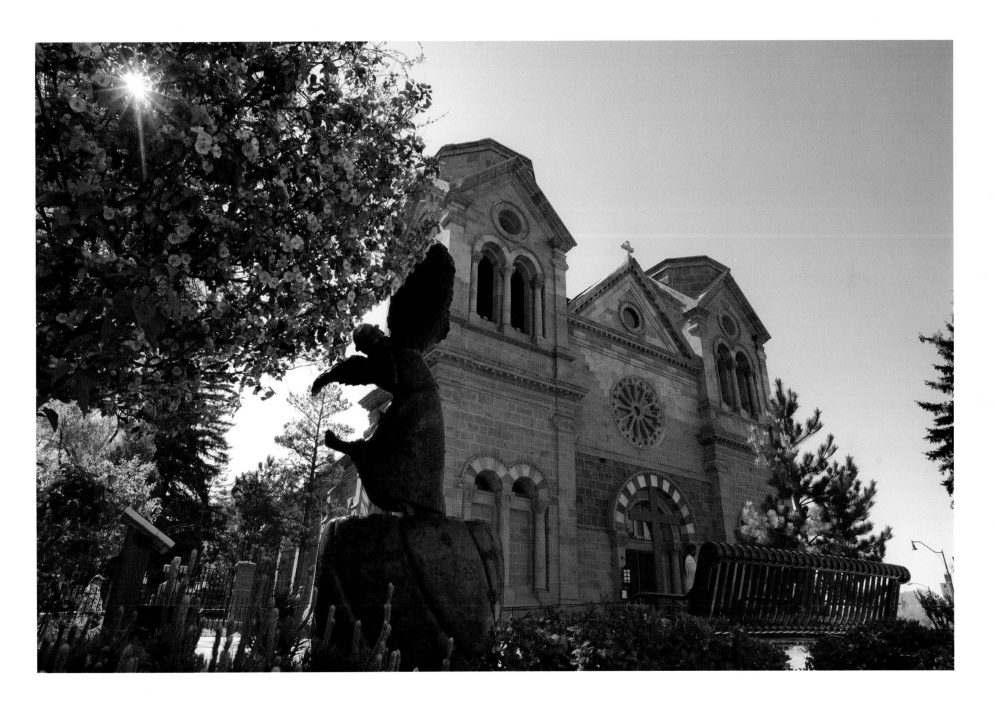

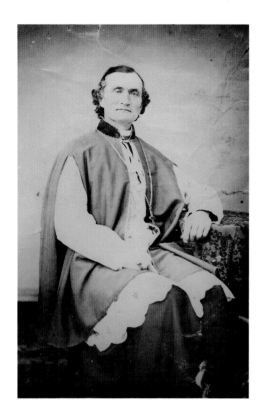

Bishop Lamy's house, now on the grounds of the Bishop Lodge Ranch Resort and Spa. In 1851 Jean-Baptiste Lamy came to New Mexico by orders of the Vatican as the first bishop of the new Southwest Diocese. He built his home, the Villa Pintoresca, in the Little Tesuque Canyon in 1853. Lamy is venerated for having established schools, social services and Santa Fe's first hospital. His chapel is listed on the National Historic Register.

Inn of the Anasazi, near the corner of E. Palace and Washington avenues.

Japanese tea ceremony at Sunrise Springs Resort and Spa.

Built in 1931, the Lensic Theater is known for its ornate Spanish Revival façade.

Next to the Lensic, Burro Alley is where firewood used to be sold. It would be filled with donkeys loaded with wood cut from the nearby mountains.

La Casa Vieja – The Oldest House –
may or may not be the oldest house in
the country, but it was built in the early
1700s and is a wonderful example of a
Spanish Colonial residence of East De
Vargas Street in the Barrio de Analco.

Interior of the Oldest House,
refurbished in 2003.

Built in 1781 west of the Santa Fe Plaza, the historic Nuestra Senora de Guadalupe church is now an art and history museum. It is considered the oldest extant shrine to Our Lady of Guadalupe in the country.

San Miguel Chapel, along Old Santa Fe Trail, is believed to be the oldest continuously used church in the United States. It was constructed in 1610.

Nuestra Senora de Guadalupe interior.

San Miguel Chapel interior.

The Spitz Clock outside of the New Mexico Museum of Art was donated to Santa Fe in 1971 by the Spitz family, owners of a jewelry store that first opened here in 1881.

Georgia O'Keeffe Museum

Morada, or lay church, at El Rancho de las Golondrinas. The collection of buildings is a living history museum 200 acres in a rural farming valley just south of Santa Fe. The museum opened in 1972 to showcase life in Spanish Colonial New Mexico. Original colonial buildings on the sitedate from the early 1700s. Other historic buildings from across northern New Mexico have been reconstructed at Las Golondrinas as well. www.golondrinas.org

New Mexico Museum of Art was built in 1917, based on missions at Acoma and other pueblos. It was built as the art gallery of the Museum of New Mexico, founded in 1909 by famed archeologist Edgar Lee Hewett, and gave area artists an outlet for their work as commercials galleries weren't established yet. This early support of the arts is credited with making Santa Fe the art mecca it is today. www.nmartmuseum.org

A re-enactor strolls the grounds at El Ranco de las Golondrina.

El Molino Grande, a grist mill transported to Los Golondrinas from Sapello, N.M.

Museum of Indian Arts & Culture

Museum Hill complex consists of the Museum of Spanish Colonial Art, Museum of Indian Arts and Culture, Museum of International Folk Art and the Wheelwright Museum of the American Indian. www.museumhill.org

Apache Mountain Spirit Dancer by Craig Dan Goseyun, on Milner Plaza at Museum Hill.

The Museum of International Folk Art at Museum Hill.

The Museum of International Folk Art displays rotating exhibits from around the world. Here, costumes from Trinidad are part of a show about carnival celebrations.

Museum of Spanish Colonial Art at Museum Hill, www.spanishcolonial.org..

Visitos to Pecos my explore the reconstructed kiva, or underground ceremonial chamber.

Museum of Spanish Colonial Art at Museum Hill, www.spanishcolonial.org.

Opposite. Pecos National Historical Park, 25-miles east of Santa Fe, preserves the ruins of Pecos Pueblo and the Spanish mission that was built there in 1625. The park also contains the Civil War battlefield of Glorieta Pass, where the Confederate Army was defeated by Federal troops and forced to retreat to El Paso, Texas.

The Allan Houser Sculpure Garden, east of Santa Fe, displays the work of this celebrated Chiricauhua Apache artist, who lived and worked in Santa Fe. This piece, *Sacred Rain Arrow,* is being used on Oklahoma State license plates. www.allanhouser.com

The Chama River is a major tributary to the Río Grande, flowing 8-miles northwest of Ghost Ranch. It was designated a Wild and Scenic River in 1988.

Christ in the Desert Monastary, 75 miles north of Santa Fe, was founded in 1964. Monks here follow the Benedictine life, some taking a vow of silence. The public is welcome to visit, and may even rent a guesthouse here. www.christdesert.org.

Ghost Ranch is where Georgia O'Keeffe explored and painted. She maintained a house here, and eventually moved to nearby in Abiquiú. She died in Santa Fe at 99. Today 21,000-acre ranch is a retreat and education center run the by the Presbyterian Church. www.ghostranch.org

Historic Los Luceros, 30-miles north of Santa Fe, was the home of Mary Cabot Wheelwright from 1923 to 1958. In 1950, Rancho de Los Luceros was listed among New Mexico's Register of Cultural Properties, followed in 1983 by National Park Service endorsement on the National Register of Historic Places.

Abiquiú morada, near Georgia O'Keeffe's home. Tours of her Abiquiú home made be arranged through the Georgia O'Keeffe Museum in Santa Fe, www.okeeffemuseum.org.

Puye Cliff Dwellings at Santa Clara Pueblo north of Santa Fe. The ruins were occupied from the 1100s to 1500s. They are now open for public tours. www.puyecliffs.com

Scenes of life from Ohkay Owingeh Pueblo north of Santa Fe.

Morada and Black Mesa, north of Santa Fe.

Bandelier National Monument's Ceremonial Cave, an hour northwest of Santa Fe. Ancestors of today's Pueblo people lived here from about 1100-1300, before moving their communities closer to the Río Grande. www.nps.gov/band/

Opposite. Painted Cave in Bandelier's backcountry.

Located south of Santa Fe along the Turquoise Trail (N.M. 14) Madrid is a picturesque arts town that began life as a mining town in the 1850s, peaking in the 1930s. It was all but a ghost town, until artists and free-spirited people began drifting into town in the 1970s to reclaim abandoned mining shacks. Today is features several colorful galleries, shops and restaurants. It was featured in the 2007 film *Wild Hogs*. Locals emphasis the first syllable to designate it from the capital of Spain. www.turquoisetrail.org

The Santa Fe Century is a 100-mile bike tour that begins and ends in Santa Fe, traveling south on N.M. 14 and returning on N.M. through Galisteo. Begun in 1985, it attracts riders from across the country. www.santafe-century.com

Once famous for its Christmas decorations in the 1930s, Madrid once again celebrates the Yule season with a ghost town twist.

San Francisco church in the mining town of Golden, along the Turquoise Trail. The church as built in the 1830s, but when the Post Office closed in 1928, Golden was all but abandoned.

The Santa Fe Plaza is often closed to traffic for special events.

Las Fiestas de Santa Fe is Santa Fe's biggest celebration. The early September event commemorates the "bloodless" reconquest of Santa Fe by the Spanish in 1692, after the 1680 Pueblo Revolt forced the Spanish to retreat to El Paso, Texas. The Spanish leader, don Diego de Vargas, promised that if he was able to successfully reclaim Santa Fe for Spain, he would hold an annual mass in Our Lady of Guadalupe's honor. The Native Americans, tired of raids by other tribes and told that they would enjoy more rights now under the Spanish, agreed to allow the Spanish to return. Every year since then, a reenactment of the *entrada* is held, and the original statue of Our Lady of Guadalupe is taken from St. Francis Cathedral and paraded through downtown Santa Fe. A proclamation is read, and Native Americans from area pueblos are invited to speak (often getting in a few good-humored digs). Afterward, the crowd enjoys food booths and dancing to live music throughout the weekend. www.santafefiesta.org (above and next 10 pages)

An actor portraying a conquistador rides through town.

La Conquistadora is presented.

La Fiesta, 1955. Library of Congress.

Sunset and Morada.

Faces of Fiestas.

La Conquistadora is carried through the Plaza.

Actors represent historic figures, including Don Diego de Vargas.

Crests of Santa Fe's original families adorn the Palace of the Governors.

LUCERO   SANTO DOMINGO PUEBLO   PERALTA

Revelers dance in Palace Avenue to mariachi music.

Mariachi groups serenade crowds through the weekend.

With great theatrics, Zozobra (also called Old Man Gloom) is condemned
to a fiery demise (left), followed by fire dancing (right).

Zozobra is a 50-foot-tall marionette designed in 1926 by Santa Fe artist Will Shuster and dancer Jacques Cartier. It was meant to offer some levity to the religious themes of Las Fiestas de Santa Fe. A crowd of thousands gathers in Fort Marcy Park, where live music entertains until dusk. People write down their troubles on pieces of paper, which are stuffed into Zozobra to be alleviated by burning. Dancers, some dress as ghosts and called glooms, swirl around the arm-flailing and groaning marionette until finally the Fire Dancer sets Zozobra alight. Blazing, the crowd cheers as their bad fortune is symbolically burned, and fireworks burst overhead.

Though not officially a part of Las Fiestas, the burning of Zozobra the evening before has come to unofficially kick off the weekend. Today it is a large fund raiser for the Kiwanis Club of Santa Fe, which now owns the rights to Zozobra. www.zozobra.com (above and opposite page)

Cowboys ride again in the streets of Santa Fe.

The Desfile de la Gente - Hysterical/Historical parade celebrates Santa Fe's history with humor during Las Fiestas weekend.

A hippee bus pays tribute to Santa Fe's counterculture past.

Madison and Faith enjoy the festivities and face painting of Las Fiestas weekend.

At the end of Las Fiestas, a Mass of Thanksgiving is held at St. Francis Cathedral, followed by a candlelight procession to the Cross of the Martyrs overlooking the city.

Zozobra lives on after his burning on this parade float.

Sangre de Cristo aspens turn color as fall comes to Santa Fe. (above and opposite)

The nearby art community of Galisteo holds a studio tour every October. www.galisteostudiotour.org

Winsor trail is considered one of the best mountain biking trails in the nation.

The Plaza in fall color.

Skeletons from Mexico help Santa Feans celebrate November's
Dia de los Muertos – Day of the Dead.

Classical Gas Museum in Embudo. Owner Johnnie Meier is active
in neon sign and Route 66 preservation throughout New Mexico.

The Río Grande north of Santa Fe is renowned for its excellent fly fishing.

With the chile harvest in, New Mexico's state vegetable (a fruit, actually) is seen everywhere in Santa Fe.

Resources

City of Santa Fe
www.santafe.gov.

Fiesta de Santa Fe
List of events and schedules for the annual Santa Fe Fiesta in September
www.santafefiesta.org.

Georgia O'Keeffe Museum
www.georgiaokeeffemuseum.org
505-946-1000

Hyde Memorial State Park
Check out conditions and activities at this Website for New Mexico state parks.
www.emnrd.state.nm.us/prd
505-983-7175.

New Mexico History Museum
www.nmhistorymuseum.org
505-476-5200

New Mexico Rail Runner
www.nmrailrunner.com

New Mexico Museum of Art
www.mfasantafe.org
505-476-5072

Museum Hill
www.museumhill.org

Museum of Indian Arts & Culture
505-476-1250

Museum of International Folk Art
505-476-1200

Museum of Spanish Colonial Art
505-982-2226

Wheelwright Museum of the American Indian
505-982-4636

Palace of the Governors
www.palaceofthegovernors.org
505-476-5100

Santa Fe Chamber of Commerce
www.santafechamber.com
505) 988-3279.

Santa Fe Convention and Visitors Bureau
www.santafe.org
800-777-2489, 505-955-6200

Santa Fe Ski Area
www.skisantafe.com
505-982-4429

The Burning of Zozobra Official Site
www.zozobra.com

Turquoise Trail National Scenic Byway
Information and history for this scenic drive on NM route 14 and communities found along the way
www.turquoisetrail.org